C0-DAO-481

Almost Home

Almost Home

Bob Gutierrez

Copyright © 2010 by Bob Gutierrez.

Library of Congress Control Number: 2010910484
ISBN: Hardcover   978-1-4535-4007-7
               Softcover   978-1-4535-4006-0
               Ebook   978-1-4535-4008-4

All rights reserved. No part of this book may be reproduced or transmitted in any form or by any means, electronic or mechanical, including photocopying, recording, or by any information storage and retrieval system, without permission in writing from the copyright owner.

This is a work of fiction. Names, characters, places and incidents either are the product of the author's imagination or are used fictitiously, and any resemblance to any actual persons, living or dead, events, or locales is entirely coincidental.

This book was printed in the United States of America.

To order additional copies of this book, contact:
Bob Gutierrez Ministries, Inc.
1-940-230-6499
P.O. Box 4
Ore City, TX 75683
Email: pastorlinda@btfdenton.org

CONTENTS

DEDICATION

I would like to dedicate this book first of all to my Lord and Savior Jesus Christ. To my precious wife Linda of 37 years of marriage whom I love and treasure. My children Lynnette and Robert BJ whom have always been there for me. My son in law Jason Hunter Bonner I. and my daughter in law Jennifer Lynn for their love and support.

To my very special grandkids Alexis 5 years, Olivia 3 years, and Jason Hunter II. 3 years. My pride and joy I love you all. Thank you for being there always.

Love,

Bob
Dad
Papa

From top to bottom Alexis (baby), Hunter and Lynnette (couple),
BJ and Jennifer (other couple),
Large picture of couple is Bob and Linda

Alexis

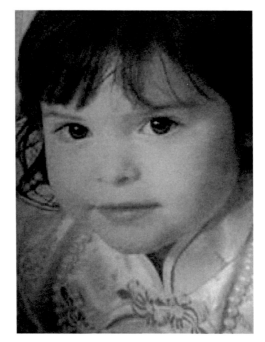

Olivia

Jason Hunter II

FOREWORD

I have been privileged to know the man of whom this book speaks for almost all his life. I was actually staying in the home of his parents when first I heard about Jesus, and at that time I made Him my Lord and Savior. Bob was less than two years old at that time.

My experience with Bob Gutierrez has been both personal and also within the parameters of his Christian service. His story and life are remarkable, and I could wish the book, which has now been written, might have been written years ago. It is a great story, but it is also a miraculous account of God's healing power in Christ. Such a story never grows old, and my sincere prayer is that hundreds may be stimulated and blessed by reading it.

I heartily recommend the book *Almost Home* to those who may have the opportunity to read it, and join many who know Bob in sending it out on the wings of faith.

Jose Leyva
Secretary-Treasurer
Central Latin American Council
The Assemblies of God
Albuquerque, NM

PREFACE

This book is not about Vietnam. This book was completed on the twenty-fourth anniversary of Bob's wounding. It is therefore an old story, but the real story is the amazing miracle that God effected in him. There will always be a need for stirring books that inspire faith and lead to divine healing. For this reason, I have written *Almost Home*. The book has been written with the prayer that it will lead to God's help and blessing in the lives of multitudes.

INTRODUCTION

When I was a little girl, my heart was often stirred by the passionate preaching of men of God, men whose lives and ministries were being greatly used to win people to Jesus Christ. In those early years, I determined to find such a man as my life partner, or remain single. The determination remained with me into my older teenage life, and while I was in Bible College, I met such a man.

The man whom I met was a man of unquestionable courage, a man in whose life God had performed a miracle of majestic dimension. He was also a man of total commitment to the Lord Jesus Christ, and a man of great preaching and singing talent. I knew he was the man God had reserved for me. You can read about our meeting in the last chapters of this book, and I am thrilled and excited to introduce you to my husband—God's servant Robert Jimenez Gutierrez. Enjoy his story as I have enjoyed my life with him.

With joy in Christ,
Linda Gutierrez

1

FLASHBACK

An unearthly silence hung over the headquarters of the military camp, a huge installation of American power. The air was heavy with acrid fumes from the explosions that had occurred only moments before. Any casual observer would have been justified in thinking that doomsday had arrived or, perhaps, that a goon squad of demolition experts had just completed an assignment.

Suddenly, the encampment came to life. Men emerged from bunkers and safety spots to gaze upon the destruction, which, after all, was not anything they had not seen before. They emerged dazed and confused, their faces grim, and their lips compressed with anger and shock. The rockets, which had slammed into their breakfast hour only moments ago, were wholly unexpected, and certainly unwelcome. The first rocket had exploded harmlessly. It had the immediate effect of sending the soldiers into shelter. Now they squinted through the haze and smoke, congratulating themselves that they seemed to be uninjured and, with the usual cynicism of war-weary troops, made lewd remarks about the enemy. They were soldiers of the United States Army, the enemies were gooks. It was Vietnam, and the date was April 15, 1969. The location was Camp Enari near Pleiku, the headquarters of an artillery battery of the Second Corps.

Bob Gutierrez never felt anything. With everyone else, he had scrambled for cover. He never made it, and the rocket that exploded directly above his head—or, perhaps, slightly to the left and above him—left him standing on his feet. Bob never uttered a sound, nor did he speak a word. A half-minute later, he crumpled to the ground. He knew he was injured. In the moments after the explosion and while he was frozen into the passing seconds, he reflected that he was without pain. He was able to see, to hear, and to think. An indescribable horror swept over him, and he was actually aware of tears in his eyes. In later years, Bob would never have sufficient words with which to define the complete hopelessness of those seconds. As he sank to the ground, he heard the voices of others. His mind framed the words, "God, please let me die," and when he raised his right hand to the area of his neck and face, there was no neck. As his vision faded, he was aware that there was blood pouring from where he thought his neck should be, and he felt that his hand had passed through to his spine.

Bob's comrades surrounded his now inert body. Those who were hardened by war and death spoke bitter expletives, shook their heads, and left. The medics took what they thought was a body to the Battalion Aid Station for disposition.

2

FOURTEEN KIDS

Ramon Gutierrez stood beside the woman who was about to become his wife. He was well satisfied with his choice, and he knew that she was a natural mate for him. His green eyes twinkled, and he threw a wink in her direction. He leaned toward her and whispered, "How many children do you want?"

Nieves looked startled. Later, when the last friend had gone, she grinned at Ramon and challenged him with the same question: "So, *mi esposo*, how many children do you want?"

Ramon chuckled, hugged her, and replied, "Just as many as the good Lord gives us, *querida*! OK?" Nieves smiled gently to herself and murmured, "I hope He feels generous, Ramon. I love babies."

A few years and three sons later, Nieves presented Ramon with yet another son. He said, "You seem determined to keep this family going, Nieves. A boy? What shall we call this one?"

"Let's call him Robert," she answered.

Ramon and Nieves added a second name, and Robert Jimenez Gutierrez was launched into life, to be known as Bob. He entered life in the City of Angels, two years after the end of World War II. It was September 8, 1947.

Bob was not the last child. Nieves got her wish, and year after year, the family grew, until fourteen children surrounded her. They were both her joy and her helpers. Ramon and Nieves were migrant field-workers, and as the children grew in understanding and ability, they took their place beside their parents in the summer harvest. In many states, from south to north and west to east, the Gutierrez family picked tomatoes, pulled lettuce, and gathered grapes and plums. They had very little of this world's wealth, but they ate fresh vegetables and fruit.

The nomad life of the family exacted a heavy toll on the parents and the children. As the children were carried to birth, Ramon sought to be patient and caring. Nieves worked as long as she was able to do so, and so the years flew by. They lived sometimes in tents and often in small, cramped, dirty shacks. On many occasions, the children observed the indignities that were heaped upon their parents. They heard them demeaned, slighted, and cursed, yet at the end of the working days, their parents gathered them together, and for a few short hours, they became a praying family.

When Bob was twelve years old, Ramon decided to establish an actual home for his children. By this time, the family included some girls, of whom there would ultimately be six. Ramon obtained a home in Stockton, California. It was extremely modest, but to Bob and the other children, it seemed palatial. After the conversion of a den to a third bedroom, the whole family settled into a somewhat normal life. Even though there was always a waiting line for the bathroom, life was greatly improved from what it had been in the earlier years.

Life in Stockton did not mean the end of fieldwork. Whenever possible, the children went to work alongside their father, and the older children often went with him as the first light of dawn broke. Life was hard, but the home gave the family a sense of belonging and togetherness.

Ramon and Nieves Gutierrez brought their children into the world as precious gifts from God. They were deeply committed to Jesus Christ and were actively part of a strong local church. They raised their children to the upbeat, heart-pulling songs of an evangelical and fervent persuasion. The message of the gospel and the music of heaven were as fundamental to them as the food they ate and the air they breathed.

What life was at the poverty level in this world was rich in fellowship with God and with those believers with whom they shared. Aching backs and tired bodies never hindered their happy hearts, nor their lilting songs. They were a happy family.

Into such a life, the fourteen children came. Over the years, every one of them, eight boys and six girls, made personal decisions to follow Christ.

Bob looked back many times in years that were still to come and thanked God for parents who knew and followed the Lord.

3

FORGET IT, KID!

In one way, the years of his teens were the hardest of Bob's life. The grinding pace of poverty in his family setting reached far into his mind and emotions. There were days of fun and laughter despite the dawn-to-dusk schedule of his experience. For the most part, however, Bob was maturing into postpuberty years with a chip on his shoulder and a thousand good promises made to himself concerning the future. There was no way, he decided, that he would ever be content with the humdrum, moneyless life of his earlier years. One brother started working in a grocery store soon after Ramon secured the house in Stockton. Bob was envious of the little wage that Xavier brought home and swore that the future would also be good to him.

"What I really want to do," he ruminated, "is become a great singer." Bob had watched the performance of many singing groups in his church, and there seemed to be a certain touch of glamour in what they did. "I can do that," he assured himself.

Bob's older brothers were already singing in the church choir. Some of them had unusual talent. Bob had a yearning to stand with them on Sundays. He figured that if he could get into the choir, there would be practices to attend, and even some trips upon which he could go. So he planned, and so he dreamed.

Bob's dreaming and figuring never put money in his pocket, however. He longed for the security of owning something on his own. Many times, he dulled the edge of his teenage Christian conscience and simply stole things that he could easily sell. He knew his behavior was wrong, and he was always sorry for the action, while at the same time enjoying the freedom to have a little money.

After a year or two, Bob persuaded the music man in the church to allow him to attend choir practice. The people all said he was too young, and not "tuneful" enough to be in the choir, but he was too excited to allow the harshness to bother him. The choir director was a family friend.

"I'm going to be a singing evangelist," Bob bragged to one of his brothers. The answer lingered in his mind for years afterward.

"Forget it, kid. You couldn't carry a tune in a bucket if it had two handles," he was told. The idea that he could not sing hurt deeply. Bob wanted so desperately to be able to sing and determined not to accept the judgment about his voice.

"I'll ask God to help me to sing. He can do anything," the boy reasoned. Bob began to pray each day for a beautiful voice. He never doubted his prayer would be answered. He was only fifteen years of age, but already, the strong biblical preaching to which he had been exposed was bearing fruit. He remembered the Bible verse that had originated in the mouth of Jesus: "If ye shall ask anything in My Name, I will do it" (John 14:14).

"One of these days I'm going to show my brothers and everybody else that I really do have a voice and I can sing," Bob insisted. His brothers and friends merely laughed and said, "Forget it . . . no way will you ever be able to sing."

At the age of fifteen, there wasn't much more a kid could do. Bob always got red in the face and spat back, "You wait! You're going to see," and regularly attended choir practice despite the ridicule.

4

THE TOUCH OF GOD

Big brother, Xavier, became the music director of his—and Bob's—church. Two other brothers, Mike and Paul, were also choir members. Bob took a deep breath and felt safer! "For darn sure, Xavier won't kick me out of the choir. I'm safe now," he figured. There were a couple of angles for which, however, he had not reckoned.

Xavier, Paul, and Mike began to practice as a trio. Bob's middle-teen mind was slow to accept their quality and increasing ministry. Xavier, partly amused and irritated, and genuinely concerned for Bob, finally asked him if he would like to join them to complete a quartet. Bob was in rapture, but the first practice was a disaster. He was unable to carry a tune, just like the folks had said. Bob became bitter and angry, and as the weeks passed, he found himself actually cursing his brothers.

Night after night, he fretted, long after the other members of the family were asleep. He screamed silently, "Why don't You hear me, God?" His misery was compounded when he inadvertently learned that Xavier's college professor in music had said, "Don't bother with Bob, he just doesn't have it." Music teachers and college professors had, in one way or the other, told him the same thing. His cup of boyish disillusionment was complete. His brothers had failed him, friends had failed him, and to all appearances, God didn't care! Then a miracle happened. As he would live to know in future years, God met Bob at the end of his road. Much later, he would know that God frequently waited to points of human need, even desperation.

Somewhere in the transition from boyhood to young manhood, God gave Bob a beautiful voice. The change did not take years. It appeared to others that one day Bob could not sing, and the next day, he possessed a lovely, tuneful, and rich voice. He was wholly overwhelmed, and out of his mouth came a stream of gratitude and of praise.

"You heard me, God! You actually heard me! I will serve You with this voice," Bob promised.

The voice given to Bob was no ordinary voice. It had a unique quality. Suddenly, he was inundated with invitations to sing. Almost as though Satan wished to divert the wonderful new gift, Bob began to receive invitations to sing with rock-and-roll groups. His voice was especially suited for that style, but from deep within his spirit came the response, "I will only sing for Jesus Christ." Years later, Bob would look back and marvel at the strength given by God, strength by which his future life for Christian service was preserved.

In the days of miracle, Bob's maturity levels soon rose dramatically. He was now a strong and virile man. In spiritual things, the days of compromise were all gone. For Bob, it was a total commitment to the claims of Jesus Christ and a dependence on the power of the Holy Spirit.

"What do You want me to do, Lord?" was the constant prayer of his life. As his seventeenth year passed by, a holy determination was born in him. Bob announced his intention to train for active Christian work. "I will go to Bible College," he said.

The administration of the Latin American Bible College in La Puente, California, accepted Bob as a student, and he, in turn, accepted the challenge of the gospel of Jesus Christ. He determined to never sing for the sake of singing. "I will sing to win people to the Savior, or I will not sing," he affirmed.

While in the Latin American Bible College at La Puente, Bob found himself automatically linking with other students who loved Christian music. There were no buckets large enough to contain the lilt and melody that continually erupted from him!

It was, however, 1966. The bloody, senseless war in Vietnam grew ever more horrible. Thousands of the best young men in the Unites States of America were being drafted to service, and perhaps to die. The smell of blood could be recognized in countless homes across the land. Bob was approaching draft age, and along with thousands of others, he was willing to do what his country required of him. Most of all, though, he wanted to serve Jesus.

Toward the end of 1966, Bob was asked to sing for a well-known group from Nashville, Tennessee. The great opportunity had arrived! Because Bob was in college, he was twice deferred for military service. In the best sense of the word, he used the school time as preparation for the ministry of music.

Early in 1967, Bob founded his first gospel singing group. In many churches around Los Angeles and as far as northern California, his gospel quartet sang its way into the hearts of the people who listened, and Bob began to see his yearning satisfied. He was finally winning people who were lost, while blessing the lives of folk who were already Christians.

During the school year, Bob was involved in a really bad car wreck. A vehicle traveling forty miles an hour faster collided with his car. At the time the accident occurred, Bob was deeply involved with a college evangelistic team in addition to his singing. His whiplash, and the continual pain in both his head and neck, compelled him to drop out of school. He viewed the time out as temporary, and with much confidence looked forward to an ongoing service in, and for, the Kingdom of God. His life had been planned out for the service of Jesus Christ.

Bob Gutierrez knew that the touch of God was in his life. He believed he was a servant of God and a true soldier in the army of the King of Kings.

5

ANOTHER ARMY

Bob began to feel much better. The throbbing pains in his head were less frequent and less severe when they did occur. The dull, persistent ache in the upper spinal column almost disappeared by the fall of 1967. "I'm going back to school," he told his parents.

"You mean Bible College, don't you?" they asked, and to their surprise he replied, "No. I expect I'll be drafted again, and it's much less hassle to be right here at home. The draft board knows I dropped out of school, and I expect it is about time for them to catch up with me. What d' ya think?"

Ramon and Nieves pondered the question. They were reluctant to lose him to Vietnam, but they were also glad to have him serve his country. "If that's what you feel, Bob," they replied.

"Yep, sure is," Bob replied. "I may as well figure to get it over with. Most of my friends are already gone, and I've had two deferments. I don't especially want to go, but I'm not trying to chicken out either."

A little reluctantly, they agreed with Bob's reasoning, and when the fall term opened in San Joaquin College, Bob was there—for better or for worse.

Two weeks after school began, a letter arrived for Bob. "It's the way I figured it," he told his mother.

With a quiet smile, he opened the envelope that was to change his life forever. Thousands of men had chuckled after opening similar letters. It claimed that the president of the United States wished to say, "Hi!" The letter bluntly said, "Greetings from the President of the United States. Mr. Gutierrez, you have just been drafted into the United States Army."

It wasn't the exact army in which Bob had planned to serve! Yet there was a certain sense of pride and relief in him. He picked up the phone and called all his closest friends, those who were still around. He wondered if he would catch up with some whom he knew were already in uniform. "Mom, I'm going to get fit in a hurry!" Basic training, marching, running, climbing ropes and jumping hurdles, learning to say, "Yes, sir!" and "No, sir!" and accepting the nose-to-nose verbal abuse that was normal for trainees.

Then, about two months down the line, Bob knew that his orders would be cut, and that after advance training in something, he would almost certainly be shipped out to Vietnam. It wasn't a time for deep reflection. It was simply something that life had dealt him. He did phrase a question to his parents, a question for which there was no clear answer.

Bob asked, "How d' ya suppose this fits in with what God wants to do in my life? I doubt the Vietcong will be interested in listening to me sing, but I would surely like to keep singing."

Nieves Gutierrez looked at her son with an almost prophetic intensity and said, "You'll sing, *mi hijo*. Wherever you go, you will sing. God gave you your voice, and He doesn't take back the gifts which He gives."

"I think you're right, *Mamacita*," Bob replied and added, "I'm so grateful for your encouragement and for your faith in me." Nieves responded quickly, "Bob, it's not so much you, my son. Rather it is what I feel God has chosen to do through you."

A day was still in the future when the words, which Nieves spoke to Bob, would provide a part of the anchors that were to hold him when everything else had slipped away. Ramon slapped his son on the back, his mother kissed him, and he went bravely down to the induction center for his area.

As he made his way to the induction center, he fell into an age-old human habit. He began to talk to himself, aloud. Doubt and uncertainty swept over him. All the cherished dreams of his youth crowded his thinking, and muttering and stuttering, he made his case to God, defensively, and part in anger.

"You see, God . . . ," he started, then stopped. He tried again. "It's not like I mind going to Vietnam, but . . ." Once again he stopped, bit his bottom lip, and rushed on. "You have called me to win people to Jesus and sing for Him. How am I supposed to do that in the army? I'll be killing people for sure."

"God, I'd like You to have me refused on medical grounds. OK? You know I had that accident, and if I don't pass the medical examination, I can go on with serving You."

Finally, Bob lapsed into silence, and then the God to whom he had talked got a moment to talk back. Bob began to hear in his spirit from the Holy Spirit, and because he knew that voice, he listened carefully.

"You must not be afraid," the still, small voice insisted. "In the same way in which I have brought you to this time of life, I will lead you again. The day will come when My mighty power will be shown through you. For now, I want you to trust Me."

At the assigned medical examination, Bob was declared, for pre-induction medical purposes, to be wholly fit. The man with the selective service number 4-33-47-857 and identified with the number 5-68-35-233 was, they said, "normal and acceptable." His final medical clearance was dated December 12, 1967. As he made his way to his parent's home, he sighed deeply, and once more talking aloud, he said, "It's OK, God. I'll try to find a way to sing, even if it is just to myself."

He was all sworn in and ready to be a soldier in this other army. While Bob understood that it would not be easy to serve the King of Kings in the army of the United States, he was willing to believe that he could do both. Men about to die needed Jesus too, he reflected.

Bob was posted to Fort Lewis, Washington, for his basic training. Along with many others, he was shorn, equipped, and secretly a little alarmed at the barking and screaming of the drill instructors who were about to be both mothers and fathers to him in this rough and tumble, other man's army.

6

UP, UP, AND AWAY!

By any man's account, the transition from the comforts of civilian life to the rigors of military life can never be disallowed or discounted. Bob was now happy for the hundreds of backbreaking hours that he had spent in the fields with his father and mother, hours in many different locations. He was not wholly devastated in the strangeness of his new life. Some aspects of army life made him cringe and long for the days of his boyhood.

Two things he knew for sure. Even while he was growing into puberty, and throughout his entire youth, filthy language was not a part of his life. Suddenly, harshly and cruelly, Bob's mind was ravaged by words that were foreign to him. It was not that the words were unknown to him, but rather that in the Christian environment of his upbringing, the use of such words was both unacceptable and unknown. He knew he was incapable of adopting the language of the barracks.

The other thing he knew for sure was that the men with whom he trained generally had a wider experience among girls and women. Perhaps because of the size of his family, he had developed with a clean untainted attitude toward the other sex. He was totally without personal sexual experience. Bob found it difficult to hear the bawdy jokes in the barracks, and the relating of sexual exploits affronted the sensitivities that had been sown into his life.

Despite these obvious differences, he related well to the men with whom he served. Sometimes, before the call for lights out, Bob sang, largely for himself. The men enjoyed his voice, and occasionally, both needled him and at the same time asked him to sing.

"Hey, Bob, how 'bout singing sumpin' like home stuff?" and Bob would always sing. He was wise enough not to impose his own sensitivity upon his buddies and, as a result, enjoyed a measure of respect and popularity among the men.

In Fort Lewis, Bob's lithe young body hardened, and he became aware of his own manhood. The protective covering of both home and church had been stripped away, and he was becoming what "this man's army" wanted him be. Additionally, his Christian life became more mature. Rather than it being something he believed, it now became something that he felt compelled to practice. After a while, he found other men who loved God and who were also in the "other man's army." It wasn't all that difficult, Bob decided.

The time in basic training passed very quickly, and Bob was almost startled to have a friend say to him one morning, "Hey, Bob! We're out of here at the end of the week." Bob realized how different he was compared to the rather soft young man who had reported to Fort Lewis six weeks previously. *What now?* he thought. The war in Vietnam was calling for men, lots and lots of men. Bob's orders were cut for artillery training, and he was posted to Fort Sill in Oklahoma. In the pressure of the time, training was intense and reduced to what was absolutely necessary. The constant noise of firing gave Bob an entirely different view of the days that were ahead of him.

"Load . . . fire! Load . . . fire! Load . . . fire!" He learned with his mates, to do it all, to alternate positions, to change trajectory, and even to vary weapons. By the time Bob was finished at Fort Sill, he was a qualified cannoneer, an old-fashioned responsibility that every war had required since the discovery of gunpowder, and even before that with the use of catapults and slings.

Cannoneer Gutierrez was good and ready to take the normal seven days of home time. "Wow!" he commented to his closest friend. "Will I ever be glad to eat some food at Mom's table. I mean, man, it'll be good to go home for a few days."

Bob discovered, along with all the other ready-to-die men, that there was a little thing still to be given out. The army called the directive final orders.

Every man who got final orders felt an uncanny kind of oppression, as though the directive was a sort of death sentence, which, indeed, for thousands of men under the age of twenty, it was. Bodies piled upon bodies in the slime of countless rice paddies, or in the impenetrable jungles of Vietnam. It was all on account of those final orders!

Bob found the seven days at home almost insufferable. When he compared notes later with his buddies, they all had felt the same way. For those who boozed and partied, the days were one long blur of wine, women, and song. For Bob, the days were deeply thoughtful, filled with nostalgia, familial love, and much prayer. The countdown was ominous. Seven, six, five, four, three, two, and then the last day was there. Bob had told his mother, "Cook me everything which we ever eat, for it will be a long time until I taste good Mexican food again." The days were filled with tamales, tacos, tortillas, came asada, and plenty of rice and beans.

The last day was poignant and emotional. While tears were very near the surface, they were countered by the quiet faith of this family. Ramon and Nieves made a massive going-away meal. The family friends piled into the available space, and with laughter and tears, pain and joy, Bob said his farewells.

Well-meaning friends asked inane things such as, "Are you ready to go, Bob?" or, "Are you excited?" It finally became more than Bob could handle, and he left them all, to be alone in the room where he always slept.

Two hours before departure, Bob asked a family member to have his father come and talk with him. In the utter quietness of the room, two grown men, father and son, looked deeply into one another's eyes. "*Mi padre*, within a couple hours I'll be leaving for Vietnam. I don't know whether I'll ever return. I'm sorry I do not have anything to give you, but I bought this watch a couple days ago, and I want you to wear it for me. It's all I have, Dad. Now it is yours." Tears rolled down Ramon's cheeks as he reached for the watch. With heavy father-grief, he said, "Son, you'll be back. You'll be back."

The little boy, whom God had supernaturally given a voice of liquid gold, picked up his things an hour or so later and turned his face to Vietnam. With hundreds of others, he boarded a plane that was routed nonstop to the bloody, killing fields, and to an unspeakable horror for which his country had assumed an obligation.

Bob knew that many of his best friends would come out of the lines in body bags. He understood there would be little time for him to think about that in Vietnam. For now, though, he thought about it.

7

SHOT AND SHELL

The seat belts were all buckled on the plane, and as it made its long approach to Vietnam, the men on board Bob's flight peered through the restricted area offered by the window to catch a first glimpse of its shores. It looked restful and very green. It seemed impossible that somewhere ahead of them, men were being blown to pieces. The landscape appeared as though it should have been a tropical wonderland. The shoreline reminds one of the Caribbean.

Bob, and, indeed, everyone on the plane, knew what was the disposition of the force. "So!" Bob reflected. "I'm a cannoneer in an artillery battery of the Second Corps, part of the Fifth and Sixteenth Artillery Battery of the Fourth Infantry Division," which, when all boiled down, meant that he knew how to load and fire bigger weapons than most ordinary grunts. Some of the men took comfort in the fact that they would frequently be far enough back to insure some degree of personal safety. Most had no knowledge of the cold facts that would be handed to them upon their arrival.

The receiving officer yelled stridently at the weary travelers: "Faaaall in!" There was some shuffling and complaining, but the man continued, "Try to remember that you are soldiers in the army of the United States. Get your eyes at least partly open. There's a war going on here, and you are part of it. You will fall out on my command, and wait in the staging area for your gear. You should have it within thirty minutes. From the staging area, follow the blue line . . . I SAID, THE BLUE LINE, until you reach the end of it. If you're lucky, I'll pick you up there. Faaaall out!"

An hour later, lugging their heavy duffel bags, the men were congregated together at the assigned place. Some soldier complained bitterly, "What a stinking, bum deal! I could use some real sleep. How 'bout it?"

Another answered quickly, "You'll be lucky if you ever get any sleep again. Man, this is Vietnam, remember?"

The officer arrived, accompanied by a sergeant who bellowed, "Stand easy," which the men were happy to do. He continued, "When your name is called, pick up your bag and form one line, ten paces forward . . . and move it. We need to get you out of here. You will be flown into Pleiku and trucked to Camp Enari to join the Second Corps."

One by one the men moved into line. *G*, as in *Gutierrez*, was seventh in the alphabet, so Bob's name came up quickly. The group was moved into smaller planes and promptly cleared for takeoff. Camp Enari was a large installation, and by the time the men had been processed and fed, many were mentally looking back over their shoulders and remembering how far they were from home. Bed had never looked so good, and when the men were finally bunked down and some degree of quietness prevailed, a mellow, rich voice broke the night. Bob was singing, "On a hill far away stood an old rugged cross/The emblem of suffering and shame/ And I love that old cross, where the dearest and best/For a world of lost sinners was slain/So I'll cherish the old rugged cross/'till my trophies at last I lay down/I will cling to that old rugged cross/ And forsake it some day for a crown."

When the last notes of the universally loved song died away, there was a moment of silence. Then someone voiced the common thought, "OK, Gutierrez! OK! We can sleep on that one," and so the rookies, fresh out of the United States of America, drifted into sleep. A little melancholia was to be expected. Bob made some big decisions that night. God had given him a very special gift, bestowed supernaturally in answer to his intense and sincere prayers. "I'm going to sing even though I am in Vietnam. I'll get up smiling and singing each day. I will let my light shine as best I can," he avowed before God.

For Bob Gutierrez, a son of a migrant field-worker in the good ol' United States, a whole new world was opening up. It certainly was not one he might have chosen had he been given the choice, but he prayed and hoped to make Vietnam a place in which he could minister as the Lord gave him opportunity. "They surely can't stop me either smiling or singing—can they, Lord?"

The men who served in Vietnam were well aware of the fact that they had exactly one year to serve in that country, and in his more optimistic moments, Bob usually estimated that he and his fellow cannoneers were fairly certain to be behind the front lines, targeting areas for which the coordinates had been carefully given. He and all his friends were about to be better instructed.

They rose to their first full day with instructions to assemble. Bob smiled and sang a little as they made their way to the briefing.

"Listen up, men," the lieutenant said. "I want you to get rid of any cotton-picking idea that because you are in the artillery, all you will have to do is to sit back and punch rounds at Charlie.

Our job is to shoot when we are asked to, and when we are not needed for that, we'll get our tails out of here and run patrol. The gooks are never far away, and our job is to search and destroy, one way or the other. If you have any questions, I'll take them now. If there are none, we'll get on with our job. Your noncoms will help you to make any later adjustments.

"Well, since you have no questions, let's gear ourselves into action. Sergeant, take over!"

"Yes, sir!" the sergeant said, and then laid out the duty rosters, training sessions, and familiarization rap times.

During that first unforgettable day, a runner made his appearance, looking, he said, for Private Bob Gutierrez. "I'm Gutierrez," Bob informed the man. "Watcha want, anyway?"

"The colonel wants to see you, Gutierrez," the runner answered. "He's the senior chaplain on base."

Bob didn't have the remotest idea what the colonel could want, but with the sergeant's approval, he left with the messenger. Bob reported in form and stood rigid. The colonel smiled ever so slightly and then said, "Be easy, soldier." Bob relaxed and waited.

"Private Gutierrez, I have a report which indicates that you sing rather well. Is that true?"

Bob was totally nonplussed. How could he have known? Who could have told him? Despite his surprise, he answered as a private should answer a colonel. Bob snapped to attention and replied, "Sir, the report is correct. Except, sir, that I only sing Christian music, sir!"

The full bird colonel gently chided Bob. "Soldier, I said, be easy. I want you to know that the music you sing is the only music that I am interested in at this time. I'm interested in whether you would like to sing in chapel, at least until you're settled. I could use the help, Gutierrez. I' m making a request, not giving an order, OK?"

Bob had eased as the colonel had asked, but he felt a little stunned and almost stammered as he answered, "Sir, I would be honored. Thank you for asking me. It will be just like being home."

The colonel gave Bob the service schedule, and in the few weeks during which the new men settled down, he was able to do what he loved best. He trained hard, and then at the time of religious services, he sang. He really felt that he had never sung so well. There was something about the whole setting that moved him. The living were still dying, the wounded were hurting, the future wasn't that bright, but Bob knew that for a short while, the Spirit of God had given him an opportunity to minister the reality of Jesus Christ in the words of Christian songs.

"Thank You, God," he breathed. "Thank You! Thank You! I am so grateful to You!"

Bob did not really know that he carried an extra joy with him during those days. The Second Corps was already running patrol, and on a number of times, contact had been made with the enemy. The front tended to be very fluid, and already Bob had been in action with the big gun. In every situation, Bob carried the peace of God with him, and the joy he felt in knowing Christ was simply seen by his buddies as happiness. It was a happiness that most of them didn't know.

At 0600 hours one morning, one of Bob's friends came to him and asked, "Bob, why is it that every day, even though we're in war, you wake up with a smile on your face, and you sing through the whole day?" It was the kind of opportunity for which Bob often prayed. He put his thoughts into language, which he believed would be easily understood. "What can I say? I've got the Man upstairs in my heart, and that's what keeps me full of joy."

The squad was becoming more and more active. Sometimes, Bob felt pain in his heart to realize that he was either loading or firing shells, which were inevitably killing men among the enemy ranks. When on patrol, he fired his rifle when he was ordered to do so. The law of control indicated that it was better to fire than to be fired upon. The enemy could always be assumed to be hidden in the underbrush. Sometimes he wondered how many men he had killed unknowingly.

At three o'clock one muggy morning, as the squad prepared to patrol the perimeter, one of Bob's buddies was deeply depressed. When Bob looked at him, he observed the tears in his eyes. "What's wrong?" Bob asked. His friend moved over to him and said, "Bob, will you pray for me?"

When Bob finished praying, his friend said, "You know, I feel so good, Bob. Please always pray for me, because I want to feel this way all the time." Bob assured him about the prayers, and then crooned a Christian song to him before they left the compound.

Whenever there was a quiet time in quarters, Bob lay on his cot and stared at the ceiling. In his deepest heart, he was still singing the gospel on the singing circuit at home. He often thought of the ways in which God had led him, and as he looked back, he wondered how he had ended in the bloody horror of Vietnam. His joy was tempered with sadness for all the bloodshed and pain in the anguished country.

8

SINGING ON THE SIDE

This story is that of a bright young American solder caught up in the ebb and flow of the war in Vietnam.

In the very nature of biographical material, there are frequently many fascinating details that should be noted, details that cannot necessarily be interwoven with the story itself. Details that, if placed in the actual story, might appear extraneous. In the story of Bob Gutierrez, some of the details are now inserted with particular reference to the quality of the singing voice with which he had been endowed.

In the turbulent months before his induction in to the United States Army, Bob had turned down an offer to be a lead-in number for the Rolling Stones. In passing up the offer of seven thousand five-hundred dollars for each appearance, Bob remained true to his conviction that his voice was a God-given gift. He believed that somehow God would bring his gift into the open.

During the time when the chaplains at Camp Enari discovered Bob's distinctive voice, they inquired whether he would like to do some music for the troops at large. Bob was approached, and he answered with excitement, "I'm ready right now!"

A personal-use-only helicopter took Bob to a mountain location where there was a recording studio and broadcasting station. For two weeks, he worked to produce music that would cheer, comfort, and encourage the troops throughout the entire sector.

This period was critical to the image that Bob had of himself. He gained assurance, poise, and great inner satisfaction. Occasionally, his memory made flights back to the days of his tuneless monotone, and he found himself wondering how God had done this amazing miracle. Those who recorded his voice in Vietnam were unstinting in their praise and freely offered their congratulations. His work gained him even more acceptance among the Second Corps.

Over the months of his Vietnam service, Bob had the unusual experience of being brought in from remote areas to sing. Veteran's Day, Thanksgiving, Easter, and Christmas, whenever there was a need for good music, Bob was pulled from duty. Inevitably, he began to dream about the future, more than ever before.

On one occasion, he was flown to Saigon to make a special recording at a government level. That was heady for Bob because, as he walked out of the studio, he ran into Hollywood jazz star Eddie London, considered one of the very top musical entertainers. At the time of the meeting, London was concluding a USO tour in Vietnam. He approached Bob and introduced himself, inviting Bob to chat with him for a while. "Bob, do you have time to stick around for a while?" he inquired.

"Sure do," Bob replied. "What do you have in mind?"

"I'd like you to hear the band," London told him. "Would you like that?"

When London saw Bob's enthusiasm, he made it possible for him to remain and listen to the world-class ensemble. "Whatcha think?" London asked him at the conclusion of the recording.

Bob was just full up. He said, "You guys are just too much!" London questioned, "Do you really think so, really?"

"Really! For sure, man, you're fantastic. There's no question about it," Bob gushed.

London was thoughtful for a brief moment, and then he said, "Bob, I got a vocalist right now whom I need to change. How would you like to be my new vocalist?"

"Are you kiddin'?" Bob challenged.

"Nope. When you get home from your tour, I got a contract for you. I want you to be my new vocalist," London responded.

Bob went back to base camp with a future that gave every appearance of being secure. *Oh, wow!* he thought. *With the Eddie London Band!* He pinched himself to determine whether he was still there. His mind was on a field trip to fame, with no road blocks. At least, not that he knew then.

Late in December 1968, the news flashed around Camp Enari that Bob Hope was in Vietnam. The commonly expressed wish was that he would come to Enari. On the twenty-fifth of December, the announcement was made that Bob Hope would indeed bring his troupe to Camp Enari. The soldiers immediately went into ecstasy. There would be music and real live American girls!

Then the word broke; Bob Hope's troupe needed one more male soloist. They needed a soldier who could sing. Bob's friends crowded around him and said, "Bob, you're the best there is, man, give it a whirl!"

"Nah, guys, I'm not in that class," Bob insisted. The men needled him until finally, he agreed to try out, and to his amazement and delight, he was chosen to be the all-American soldier-boy soloist.

Before thousands of American soldiers, and with his knees literally knocking, Bob Gutierrez had his moment of ultimate excitement. For that moment, he was in fact, a part of the Bob Hope Christmas Special. He sang "Oh, Holy Night" without the assistance of any music. His voice was true, and Bob felt the exaltation of the music in his spirit. He was wholly overwhelmed, and thunderous applause split the night air for an unusually long time. Bob felt both humbled and proud. It was a moment in the sun for him. One purely unforgettable experience.

The response to Bob's singing was so complete that on the following Sunday, he was asked to repeat the song. When the day ended, and Bob tried to evaluate his trip to Saigon, the meeting with Eddie London and the Bob Hope connection, he came to a conclusion. "I'm going to Nashville," he determined, and he was comfortable with the decision. He knew for sure that even the memories of the kid, who couldn't hold a tune in a bucket with two handles, were finally erased. Bob could sing, and he knew it. He reminded himself of his commitment to sing only for Jesus Christ, and he made the commitment again. He was a little uneasy about Eddie London, but he decided to leave that decision until he was home in the United States of America.

9

WALKING WITH DEATH

Bob's life in Vietnam was as intense as it was possible to be. Camp Enari remained his base, but most of the time, he and his fellow cannoneers were moving with the infantry. The action was sometimes as far as two hundred miles to the north. The normal custom was to truck forward to within five or six miles of the front line, and then dig in. The monstrous 155 mm cannons were almost as big as a tank, and they lumbered forward with their own self-propulsion. Each carried a .50-caliber antiaircraft machine gun on top. When in position, they were an awesome weapon. When the infantry called for an artillery strike upon given coordinates, the response was immediate and devastating to the enemy.

There were occasions when even in the grim heat of battle, the men of the Second Corps had opportunity to be glad. One morning, the Second was laid back with no immediate expectation of action. Near noon, the wires began to crackle, and the call came for a heavy concentration of artillery fire at given coordinates. A helicopter observer had detected a whole company of the enemy, seated and quietly eating their meal. The big guns roared into action, lobbing their ninety-seven-pound shells right on the target. Few could have escaped the intense firepower of the 155 mm guns. It just was not the right time for lunch!

Most of the time, the Second Corps was requisitioned for night barrages. This was the normal way in which to soften the enemy positions for a dawn strike by the infantry. To this extent at least, the cannoneers fought their war by a kind of remote control, but it wasn't always so. The front was mostly fluid and widespread, and when the infantrymen were not moving forward, the cannoneers were frequently asked to run patrol, to safeguard against infiltration. Plugging the holes was important, and the men of Bob's group were often asked to do so.

The call for ten volunteers came more often than the Second Corps liked, and the patrols were defined as "target practice for Charlie." Bob volunteered on one call and wished later that he had not been so willing. As the men prepared to move out, someone suggested that Bob sing. "It'll have to be a quick one, because we're likely to get our tails shot off if I make noise out there," he answered before he sang.

The patrol lined out over a distance of about two hundred yards. Cautiously, the men advanced to the underbrush that fronted the tree line. Bob felt an unusual apprehension, a chilling in the back of his neck.

"Cool it, Gutierrez," he whispered to himself. "Keep your eyes peeled!" It was his first gut-level experience of that deadly sixth sense of which others had told him. Bob knew there was trouble ahead, but to break the advance was impossible. He would have been a sitting duck by himself. He felt death in the air.

Bob broke the brush with his rifle and bayonet. An enemy soldier was simultaneously scrambling to his feet and reaching for his weapon. Back in basic training, the instructors had drilled into him the first law of survival: get him first, or he'll get you.

This was the first survival situation in which he had been placed. Bob moved quickly, fractionally to the left and then with a rapid thrust, impaling the man on his bayonet. He looked down at the dead man, and openly said, "Dear God! I've just killed my first man." He was not in shock, for he knew his 155 mm cannon had killed scores, even hundreds. However, it was the firsthand engagement, and he was grateful for the training by which he remained alive. "I suppose," he reflected, "that it had to happen sooner or later."

The lieutenant commented, "You did just fine, Gutierrez, just fine. That's one less we've got to get, and one less who can get us. I remember the first gook I killed. It's not a good feeling, but you'll be OK by the morning."

Despite the promise of this officer, Bob was still feeling squeamish in the morning. He didn't jump to volunteer on the next call, and one of his buddies commented, "It kind'a makes it a bit harder to sing, don't it, Bob?" Bob agreed and said, "I guess killing will never be easy for me, but believe me, I'll sing again."

As the front lines swept back and forth, and the big guns roared, his first face-to-face killing was soon pushed into the background of his mind, and he then smiled and sang again. It helped him to pass the mental barrier when one of the men said a few days afterward, "Bob, if you hadn't got that gook, and he had gotten you, he might easily have taken us all out. We owe you."

Bob was back on patrol again. The infamous Tet offensive was being contained, and the front was becoming normalized. Bob had not been required to kill again, and life was as near normal as the circumstances permitted. The 155 mm cannon kept banging away.

One morning, Bob was introduced to a horrifying experience when on patrol. His lieutenant was running the group in fairly close line as the squad approached the tree line. Suddenly, out from the brush ran a little boy, two, maybe three years old. The patrol froze, but the child kept coming. Obviously, the actions of the men indicated unwillingness to kill a child! The squad instinctively turned toward their officer. The child kept running and waving. The lieutenant ordered, "Hold your fire," and then, quietly determined, raised his own rifle and blew off the head of the little boy.

The men gathered quickly around their officer, and one of them said, "My God, sir, did you have to do that?" The officer said, "Follow me," and he made his way to where the boy was lying. "Men, don't come any closer. Just watch me." The lieutenant moved gingerly to the corpse and, with the end of his bayonet, very gently spread the clothing of the child. Strapped to the body were numbers of high explosive charges. "Those bastards probably told him to run toward us and we would give him candy. He was a walking ammunition dump."

"If we had let him come on, one of you would most likely have touched him, or even lifted him up. The contact detonation devices might well have blown us away. Don't ever think I wanted to kill that child. I've got one about his age at home, but this is war, and the Vietcong play by different rules. I had a decision to make . . . his life or yours. So you're still alive. I have two tours of Vietnam behind me, and I've seen worse than this. I'm only glad my decision proved to be correct. It's OK if you feel bad, but be grateful you are alive."

"Let's get out of here, OK?" Very subdued and badly shaken, the patrol returned to base. The criticism toward the officer naturally died. One soldier spoke what was in every mind, "I'm glad he knew the gook rules!"

10

ELEVEN MONTHS AND COUNTING

The Vietnam conflict was unlike any war in which the United States had ever participated. Tens of thousands of young men were processed through the system, served their country with courage, and never really knew why they were fighting. Heroes were made in Vietnam, but very few men had much love for the battle.

The struggle was, in some ways, weighted in favor of the Vietcong. Over long bloody years, the people of the land had reduced the strength of France when it was the occupying power. The people of Vietnam were totally at home in the obliterating density of the jungles and were masters of concealment and natural survivors. In the rancid and putrid forests, among snake infestation and scores of other disagreeable things, the men of the United States tried to win a war, the real causes of which they knew virtually nothing. The enemy had a constant tactical advantage. He could melt into the background of any area and emerge without ever having betrayed his identity. The man who cut the hair of a soldier one day might very well be the man who cut his throat on the following day. No way was ever found by which a Vietcong sympathizer could be recognized from one who was not. With the experience of the years, the assistance of the terrain, the camouflage of the jungles, and the absence of any normal fighting code, the enemy had frequent advantage.

Recognizably, the men of the United States had vastly superior technology, logistical skill, and weaponry. The vast resources of a mighty superpower were lined against the relatively primitive armor and equipment of North Vietnam. The forces of the United States did not lack courage or bravery. They were locked in a titan struggle in a war they were not given the right to win. Such is the verdict of history.

In Camp Enari, the men of the Second Corps were not basically different from other men in other branches of the service. They griped and complained, fought and died, just as others. One basic difference existed between the frontline infantry and the artillery behind them. On the front, the men were required to remain finely edged all the time and were consumed with the intensity of the action. Back among the 155 mm cannons, there was frequent mental stagnation caused by sheer futility. The men in Second Corps, and indeed in all artillery units, were constantly given busy work in order to occupy their time and energy.

Bob Gutierrez and his friends were the victims of the lassitude that was common in Vietnam. The only way in which they were able to cope with the endless hours of boredom was in the never-ending card games and, for those who indulged, the use of marijuana. For much of the activity, Bob did not participate. His early training precluded the use of drugs.

Their lieutenant tried to keep them busy with a series of perimeter patrols, and these ranged over large areas. The men called themselves human guinea pigs, for much of the activity seemed pointless.

From their base camp at Enari, they ranged as far as the Cambodian border, simply filling in time. Even in areas from where the infantry front had moved, Bob's group still fought an invisible enemy.

Commonly, one of the Second Corps would ask, "What's with today, Lieutenant?" and receive the classic answer, "I'm working on it!" Many of the patrols were for no other purpose than to keep the soldiers from the serious threat of boredom.

Bob continually marked off the days on his calendar. The months were slowly passing, and as the twelve-month hitch grew to its midway point, Bob felt as if he had crested a hill and was coasting homeward. As he waited, the common make-believe continued.

"Listen up, men," the lieutenant constantly said. "We're going out looking for gooks. We'll be out for ten days. Be ready to move in one hour. Check your watches. It is 0800 hours, and we move out at 0900." The men scrambled, and by 0900 hours, all the 155 mm cannons, the tankers, the food and water trucks, and the jeeps were headed out.

Looking for gooks became a euphemism for filling in time. Occasionally, they zeroed in on an enemy platoon whose coordinates had been called in. By the same token, there were heavy artillery strikes when required, but the most of the time was spent in cruising the alleged perimeters and shooting at nonexistent men of the enemy forces.

"Gooks suspected in the underbrush at 1 o'clock, Sergeant. Range five hundred yards. Commence firing at will."

"Yes, sir, Lieutenant!" and the sergeant would bring his firepower to bear until the section of undergrowth was destroyed.

Bob, having by the halfway point of his hitch, been given corporal's stripes, sometimes asked, "What were we trying to do today, Sergeant?" and a typical reply would be, "We were obeying orders, Corporal!"

Thousands of gallons of fuel, and thousands of rounds of ammunition for both the 155 mm cannons and the .50-caliber machine guns were used in what were basically play drills. The game had the result of keeping the men on their toes, and the added benefit of permitting the Vietcong spy chain to know that the rear was always ready.

The days passed by. The weeks became months, and one day Bob woke up to the fact that he only had two more weeks in the field. It would soon be time to begin to pack at Camp Enari.

"Where, for heaven's sake, have the months gone?" he asked his buddies. Some of them had shipped into Camp Enari with him, and after he asked his question, there was a burst of laughter from all of them.

"Goin' home! Goin' home!" they chorused. "They are going to turn us loose. Whoopee!"

Bob had taken two breaks on R&R, but the short days did nothing except break the monotony of the war. Now, he was going home, unhurt and terribly excited about picking up his singing ministry as soon as he was discharged. Going home!

Six days before the end of his tour in Vietnam, Bob was sent back to base. He walked around in a daze. He had served eleven months and twenty-five days, and the final five days had arrived. From now, it was downhill all the way back to the United States. Nothing, but nothing could stop him now.

That night, he sang. The men who were going home with him shared the joy. The men who were staying behind grew misty-eyed.

One guy said, "You're a Jesus freak, Bob, but it's been good having you with us. Maybe that's why we haven't been hurt. Anyway, go home and do your thing. We'll be coming on behind."

The 361st day was breaking, and Bob rose to meet it with joy. "Five days!" he shouted, "and I'm out of here."

11

DAY 361

Bob sat on the side of his bed and began to laugh. The men who were with him grinned in empathy for it was traditional to be happy for any man who was going home. Anyone of the men would have gladly taken Bob's seat on the plane out of Pleiku!

There was Jim. Jim had been real close to Bob on account of a three-way correspondence that had developed over the months. Jim's mother in Biloxi, Mississippi, had taken a keen interest in what her son had reported about his "singing friend," and in each of her letters, there were kind thoughts for Bob. She was a member of the *Mike Douglas Show* and planned to arrange an opportunity for her son's buddy to meet her boss, maybe get him a singing spot with Douglas's group.

Then there was Steve. Of all Bob's friends, he was the closest. They had traveled the whole way together. Steve wasn't enjoying the prospect of saying good-bye, but for the moment, they laughed.

"Do you think you can fly the plane home without ditching it, Bob?" Steve joked.

"You better believe I can fly 'er . . . all the way to the United States," Bob responded.

Steve and Bob grew silent, and appraising one another across the confined space, Steve said, "Bob, it won't be much fun without you."

Bob was too moved to speak. The intensity was broken by the breakfast chow arriving. By mutual consent, the moment passed, but Steve knew that Bob was more eloquent by his silence than by any reply he might have offered.

The men munched their way into the GI breakfast, letting the heightened emotions subside. "Aw, shucks," Bob blurted out between swallows, "I'll see ya' back home soon, buddy, right?"

"Right. Right, I guess so," Steve replied. "Maybe you'll be singing in the *Mike Douglas Show* by the time I get in." They both grinned and eased the personal moment away.

Bob tried for lightness. "Steve, if I had made the transfer into the Green Berets, we might never have seen one another again!"

"Chicken!" Steve joshed. "You passed every test, and then wimped out because they told you about the parachute jumps, right?"

"Right, but at least I'm gettin' outa here, and I don't really want to come back anyway." Bob laughed again and began to clear the breakfast debris.

That was when it happened. It never should have occurred. After all, Camp Enari was a base camp with its perimeters well established.

The Vietcong made it happen anyway. History says it happened, the War Department and the Pentagon say it happened.

Steve knew it happened, and for sure, Robert Jimenez Gutierrez knew it happened. It was one isolated moment in history, but it changed Bob's life, forever.

Boooom!

Steve and Bob were stunned by the shock wave of the explosion, apparently close by. They rose shakily, staring at one another in total disbelief. They were both experts in detonation recognition, and the explosion had Charlie written all over it. Their minds were stampeded by a myriad of questions as they sat down again. "Beats me," Steve said.

Boooom! Boooom! The resumption of breakfast responsibilities was rudely interrupted. Steve said, "Let's get outa here. We're being attacked."

"Nah, man, let's get this cleanup finished. There ain't no way gooks could have gotten inside the perimeter," Bob insisted.

Boooom! Boooom!

Bob and Steve concluded that despite all reasonable assumption, Camp Enari was, indeed, being attacked. Bob agreed, "Let's get outa here," and they scrambled from the eating area, intending to hit the bunkers that were located nearby.

The Vietcong had breached the perimeter of Camp Enari, and a heavy rocket and mortar attack was under way. Bob said, "Let's get our weapons, Steve, and our helmets."

As the two men emerged into open space, it was vividly clear that a real attack was under way. Rounds were bursting in all directions. Bob and Steve ran for a little bridge over which they needed to cross to make their own quarters.

Steve made the bridge, and died. In a world-stopping microsecond, Bob knew two distinct things. He knew that he was coming off his left foot and that his right foot was running for the end of the bridge. While his right foot was in the air, he also recognized that a round was coming in directly above him. To the right of him were the 155 mm cannons to which he was accustomed. In that moment of time suspension, two massive explosions took place. The enemy 122 mm round exploded, and in the same instant, gun crews on the 155 mm cannons blasted off the first counter rounds.

The indication gained by others, men near at hand, and medical authorities thereafter, was that the enemy shell burst above Bob and slightly to his left. There must have been dozens of shell fragments that wholly spread over Bob, but only one had his name on it.

Bob knew that in some way he was directly under the influence of the exploding round. He felt no pain and was left standing on his feet. That in itself was an incongruity; it was as though he were literally in the eye of a hurricane, a description that might have been considered actual if one lonely, marauding shell fragment had been somewhere else.

In the split second of the incident, Bob was not blown to the ground. He could see, hear, and think. An incredible vision sped across his mind, and he saw the picture of a funeral parlor, with his body on display in a wooden casket.

Bob's wound was an appalling interruption to his life. He was fully aware of this, and yet remained standing on his feet. He never knew for how long he stood, but in that brief period, he felt frozen into time, and yet there came a sensation for which words had never been created. Bob felt as though his blood and all of his internal organs were literally bubbling and boiling, but there was no pain.

The shell fragment that hit Bob entered his left neck below his ear, penetrated downward under the tongue, and exited in an upward twist to the right side. The fragment severed vital blood channels, and what Bob felt was the gurgling, rushing blood flow. To his perception, his insides and blood were boiling.

Finally, Bob collapsed on the ground. He was still in no pain, but intuitively, he understood that he was dying. His mind screamed out to God, "Please let me die!" But no sound left his mouth. "Lord, if it's Your will." He mentally added, *Please!*

Bob felt warmth as he lay on the ground. He raised his right hand to feel his neck, and there was no neck! In a million-to-one-type wound, Bob felt his hand slip through his neck to the other side, much as though there was no neck at all. His blood was pulsing out of him, warm and red. Then he became aware of a buddy kneeling beside him.

Tears streamed down his friend's face as he said, "Bob, Bob, you're going to be all right. You're going to be all right!" As the man tried to comfort Bob, God caused yet another vision to cross his mind. He saw Jesus Christ on the cross at Calvary and experienced a moment of blinding understanding as to the pain and suffering of the Master. Then, in the violent, loud silence of his soul, the great hymns of faith came streaming to him. The song that lingered was "The Old Rugged Cross" and especially the words "Until my journey at last I lay down," and all the time, his blood pumped out onto the ground, and his life ebbed away.

12

PRONOUNCED DEAD

One of the most distressing features of the war in Vietnam was the constant intrusion of the enemy into what were considered safe areas. Friendly and unfriendly Vietnamese all looked the same. The infiltration of the perimeter, which occurred when Bob was wounded, demonstrated again how difficult the struggle really was.

The redeeming feature was that good medical facilities were close. An ambulance was quickly at the scene, and medics did an emergency tracheotomy with a small combat can opener. Bob was still conscious and was not in pain. The Battalion Aid Station called in a helicopter, and within minutes, he was at the Seventy-first Evacuation Hospital and rushed into surgery.

The doctor approached the operating table and began to cut away the bloody clothing. Suddenly he said, "Hold the IV. This man is dead. He's stopped breathing!"

Bob was not dead. He heard each word the doctor said, and a feeling of desperation gripped his mind. In thought, he screamed, "I'm not dead! I'm not dead!" In the horror of that moment, he felt two strong hands on his back. He was aware that God was there, and for an unknown reason, perhaps under divine compulsion, the doctor swung by for a final confirmation of his death verdict. As in any such case, when he saw the signs of life in Bob, everything and everybody went into top gear. The medical team did all the preliminary things in a hurry. Bob was hooked up to an IV and to a direct bloodline. By the time the IV was in place, Bob had finally slipped into unconsciousness, not to become conscious again for a number of days.

"My God, I don't believe what I'm looking at!" the doctor said. The appalling nature of the wound was intensified with each moment of the initial procedure. The scope of damage could be correctly seen.

The frontal view of Bob's neck looked as though a blunted knife had sawn across with the two ear lobes as the points of origin and destination. The horrible gash caused by the rocket fragment was so wide that Bob had felt his hand had actually passed through his own neck. Major blood routes were severed, and indeed, Bob ought to have died.

The team of doctors worked on. To their dismay, the bleeding was so intense that fifteen units of blood were required before their work was done. Their procedures were complicated by the fact that the emergency breathing pipe had been inserted in a wrong position, causing serious damage to an already traumatized area. They discovered as they worked that the twelfth cranial nerve at the base of the tongue was totally destroyed at both left and right entrances, thus rendering the tongue wholly inert. It had become a slab of meat lying in the mouth. Bob would never again be able to swallow, speak, or spit—even if he lived. (At the time of this writing, more than twenty years later, a highly qualified doctor read the medical records in the author's presence and, slowly shaking his head, indicated that the conditions described above should all be the same.) All Bob could look forward to was a lifetime of silence and liquid food.

Among the matters that required attention on the operating table were extreme loss of blood, shock, an extended and gross wound, repair of main blood lines, wiring of the fractured right angle of the mandible, removal of the avulsed twelfth nerve and repair of the larynx—damaged by both the shrapnel and the tracheotomy, the removal of the submaxillary gland, and the insertion of a laryngeal stent to prevent future webbing in the area of the vocal chords.

When Bob regained consciousness some days later, his first significant thought was, *Will I ever sing again?* Since Bob had no way to express that question, he used his hands to express his desire for writing materials. His doctor brought what he needed, and Bob asked, "Will I ever sing again?"

The doctor looked at Bob and said, "It's too soon to say anything right now. You have been severely wounded." Bob asked for a mirror, and was given one.

What Bob saw in the mirror was something that he would never forget. His face appeared to be the size of a basketball, and the right side of his face, while bandaged, was paralyzed. The doctor told him the extent of his injuries. Somewhere under all the bandages was a shattered jawbone, a throat that had been cut from ear to ear, and other massive injuries, the future prognosis for which the doctor would say nothing.

"Dear God," Bob thought, "I asked You to let me die when I was hit. Why didn't You let me die?" He looked at the numerous wires and these to which he was attached, and his heart was troubled. He was being fed with tubes, kept alive with tubes, getting IV sustenance by tubes, and he longed to die.

A few days later, he was transferred to a hospital in Okinawa and, after more surgery, was evacuated to Letterman Army Medical Center (LAMC) in San Francisco. It was May 5, 1969.

Bob was home, a little late and not in the form or style to which he would have aspired.

13

THE LIVING DEAD

The earthly remains of Robert Jimenez Gutierrez lay on the operating table at Letterman military hospital in San Francisco. Those remains were alive, but in the first place, nobody thought they should be, and in the second, the medical team around the table had no real belief in their ability to do more than tidy up the mess that had been consigned to them. As far as their most optimistic opinions were concerned, they just knew that what was on the table would never be able to swallow, eat, spit, or talk.

Good doctors worked on Bob, some of the best the army possessed. They had studied the medical records that accompanied Bob with great care. They observed that this tough little Mexican American had not only beaten the initial death wound, helped by fourteen units of blood, but he had also thrown off a threatened attack of pneumonia in the first five days.

"What can we do for him?" the assisting surgeon asked. His senior looked into his eyes, shrugged his shoulders, and, with the protection of the anesthetized silence, replied, "Not much of anything. We can clean him up some. He'll walk out of here someday, but he will probably not thank us later. His body is sound, so we'll do what we can. Let's begin."

When Bob arrived at Letterman, he had already lost sixty-two pounds. He had been sustained totally by intravenous drip, and the real fat and flesh was gone from his body. His ribs protruded and his hands were almost those of a skeleton. His eyes were far back into his head; he was a human parody.

At the time of his arrival, his older brother Xavier was waiting at the hospital. When he was finally permitted to see Bob, he broke into tears. "Is this my brother?" he murmured to himself. He leaned over Bob and spoke his love, uttering some of the greatest words that could have been spoken. "Bob, God is good!" and again, "Bob, God is good!"

Following the first cleanup procedure, there were other surgeries. The days passed like bad dreams in a hideous reality. Bob was compelled to be in a sitting position for seven months. Tubes and wires ran in and out of his body, and for months he took up to nineteen shots a day. What was inserted simply ran out as quickly as it was given. Bob longed for death and even thought of somehow taking his own life.

The Gutierrez family was constantly beside Bob's bed. Friends came and sat with him, but he gave little response to any of them. Then he was told that one of his little brothers had commenced a singing group, and a spark of life appeared. He asked for pen and paper and wrote, "Will they please come and sing for me?" When they agreed to come, a little light shone in Bob's eyes. When the group finally came to sing, Bob was able, that night, to sleep. In his mind he said, "Even if I'm messed up, my brothers are working for the Lord." He was, for the moment, consoled.

Finally, the day came when the doctors decided to take the tubes out and the wires off. For almost a year, Bob's mouth had been wired closed, and for long months, he had been fed through a tube in his nose. Even the doctors dared a little, hoping that there might be some improvement upon their darker prognoses.

Some even suggested that Bob might function normally. When the unhitching was finished, Bob was unable to open his mouth. When, weeks later he finally began to flex his jaws, there was absolutely no movement of his tongue, and he could make no sound.

God, I want to die, I want to die, he thought. *I can't live like this. I just can't, and I ask You to let me die. Please, God!*

One day, the doctor sent for Bob. Thin like a rail, he made his way down to the clinic. "Bob," the doctor said, "we're going to have to put a tube back in you so that we can get food into you."

"But, Doctor," Bob wrote, "I can't move my tongue, so I can't eat, and I don't want a tube in my nose again." The doctor told Bob that he was ordering another full examination. It was not one that Bob would ever forget, because as a result of it, in addition to the pain, the doctors decided to expose the whole facts to Bob, but first, they wanted to do another surgery! Bob agreed for them to do the additional oral surgery. Later they called him in for conference.

"We've done all we can, Bob. We don't really know what the future development will be for you. In the meantime, we are going to make it possible for you to take liquid food. We want to confirm to you that the nerves which control your tongue are completely gone."

Bob struggled with the liquid food program and, with great difficulty, was able to master a way to let the fluids move down his throat. Then came the day when the doctors had agreed to send him home. Bob had part of the living dead for fifteen months. He was still unable to move his tongue; it continued as a slab of meat in his mouth. Bob had very limited capacity to open his mouth, and his neck and jawline were scarred and discolored. He had not gained weight either. It was some going home day!

Bob wrote a note to his nurse on the day he was scheduled to be discharged. It was brief: "Nurse, I'd like to see my doctor." The doctor, the nurse said, was too busy to come and see him.

He wrote again, "Please, Nurse, I really want to see my doctor. I've just got to see him!"

"OK, Bob, go back to your room and I'll try to reach him and see if he can see you," she replied. Bob wearily turned away and went back to his room.

Three hours later, the doctor had not yet arrived, and Bob gave up hope of seeing him. Weak and emaciated, he decided to leave. As he broke the doorway, the doctor finally appeared. With his hand, Bob asked the doctor to be seated while he wrote a message for him. It was not brief, and it was the cry of a live man who would much rather have been dead. The words he wrote were etched indelibly in his memory.

"Doc, I am tired, very, very tired. I'm begging you and pleading with you. Please, Doc, tell me, what is going to become of my life? What is in the future? Doc, is there any hope for me?"

The doctor, veteranized and professionally hardened, read the pathetic note. His head slowly bowed, and he began to weep. Big, salty tears dropped to the floor. After what seemed an eternity to Bob, he raised his head and looked Bob square in the face, the tears continuing to flow. When, at last, the doctor gained a measure of emotional control, he spoke quietly, and at some length.

"Bob, we have said very little to you, because we were afraid that the slightest thing we said might make you give up, and then you would never have made it.

"Soldier, we even told your family not to discuss your future with you. Professionally, I should not talk with you now, but let me ask you something. If I were to tell you what you want to know, do you think you would be strong enough to take it?"

Whatever color there was in Bob's face blanched away. *God,* he thought, *It must be terrible.* Yet within a moment or two, he looked eye to eye with the doctor and nodded affirmatively.

The doctor began hesitantly, but once he started, he laid out the facts.

"Bob, we have done everything that can be done, and we have tried everything which can be tried, and there is nothing more we can do for you.

"During the last exploratory surgery, we were compelled to pull your tongue out from far back in your throat. We established that earlier opinions were correct. The nerves which controlled your tongue movement are completely severed.

"You'll remember that we had the best specialist from Japan, one from Washington DC, and the best man who was available here. We made a unanimous judgment. If you should continue to live, you will be a complete mute as long as you are alive. You will never be able to speak another word.

"We know, Bob, that you were in gospel music, but you must know that you will not sing again." The doctor paused and evaluated Bob's ability to absorb what he was saying.

Bob had sagged emotionally and had sunk back in a chair. He related years afterward that at that moment he really felt as though his heart was bursting. He experienced a desolation and an unspeakable mental pain.

"That's not all, Bob, do you want me to continue?" Bob weakly nodded his head. He figured at that point that he may as well know it all.

"The thing you must know, Bob, is that you will never be able to eat like a normal person. We could sew an artificial stomach into you, to which you could have access from the outside. You would literally place the food into its mouth. It would enable you to go out with your friends, sit at the table and place food in the opening for digestion. I'm truly sorry, Bob, but I think it really is best for you to know all the facts."

Bob slowly stood up, his grief and despair written on his face. The doctor asked him to sign certain papers attesting to the uniqueness of his medical condition. It was no comfort to Bob to know that he had made medical history!

Since Bob could make no sound, the screaming he did was all in his mind. He screamed and screamed and screamed some more. *Wasn't it enough, God, that You took my voice? Why my eating? What is it that You want from me, God?*

Robert Jimenez Gutierrez was one of the men who, as a result of the horror of war, had become part of the living dead.

After the doctor had left him, Bob unashamedly wept. Great, convulsive sobs tore at him. As though he were on automatic replay, Bob relived the two occasions when he had longed to take his own life. At the time when the doctors had taken the wires away, and when Bob felt the pain of opening his mouth, he had first determined to end his life. He looked out the window and mentally prepared to jump to his death. Actually, he was making the first movement toward that end when he was brought back to reality by a quiet and insistent voice, a woman's voice.

"Bob, don't do it, don't do it. It's just not worth it. What's wrong, Bob?" Bob was startled back to normality, and when he turned around, he saw a nurse with an exquisitely sweet face. She smiled and then continued, "Bob, you must have patience. Have patience, Bob! It will happen. It really will happen!"

The woman disappeared. Sick and desperate though he was, Bob felt goose bumps all over his body. The woman did not work in the hospital, and Bob had never seen her before. Her words were tender, loving, and firm.

A few weeks later, when once again Bob had determined to end his life, and when he was opening the window to jump, the lady returned. Urgently, but quietly, she asked, "Bob, what's wrong? I told you to be patient. You must be patient. I told you it would happen. Bob, I give you my word, it's going to happen."

Following these words, the woman began to console Bob with loving promises from God. A great peace entered his heart, and then she was gone again. An angel of God had come twice to Bob, a true messenger from heaven. Months had gone by, however, and in the pain and horror of the doctor's frank evaluation, Bob had not remembered the messenger, at least not until the rerun was completed.

Then he remembered, cried out to God, and his God heard him.

14

BACK-TO-BACK MIRACLES

Before Bob checked out of Letterman hospital, he passed through a new experience that placed him in a better spiritual relationship than he had known before. There had been progressive, high spots in his life before Vietnam. His light had burned brightly in his army life, but the figurative hell through which he traveled from the day of his wounding—April 15, 1969—had drained him. For fifteen months, his mind was caught up in a ceaseless battle of survival, a total battle of body, soul, and spirit.

When the doctor left him, Bob reached a low point, lower than he had known previously. In the next hour, Bob wrestled with his God. During that time, he clearly remembered his earlier desires to take his own life, and he recalled every word that the angelic messenger had spoken. *I'd like to do that, even now*, he thought. The mental dialogue that began was all in his thoughts, for he had no power to utter one word.

God, I'm leaving here in about an hour. There is nothing for which I should go home. The doctors say my condition is permanent, and all I'm going to be is a big problem for my family. Since I will never speak again, and because I will never be able to eat, there doesn't seem any reason for me to live.

"Why didn't You let me die when I asked You? I would have been much better off. I know that You sent a messenger to talk with me when I was going to jump from the window, and sent her back later to again persuade me not to give up, but it's different now. Now I know what is ahead of me. God, I just want to die.

Bob walked over to the window and stared at the street far below. *It would be so easy,* he thought. *So very easy. Just a second or two, and then nothing.*

As the conflict raged within him, he was aware of a great and evil force directing him. "Go ahead and do it!" a powerful voice indicated. "You remember that you wanted to sing? I'm telling you that you will never sing again, and if you live, it will be only sorrow and grief for you and for your family."

As Bob reached out his hand to open the window, yet another voice spoke. Although he saw nobody, the voice had the same quality as that of the lady who had twice appeared to him. It was quietly insistent, not loud, nor strident, "Remember, Bob, I gave you my word that it would be all right. You listened then, and I want you to listen now. It is going to be all right!"

Bob turned as though to see the speaker and, finding no one, marveled at the two differing voices.

He felt the different qualities in the voices. The first was peaceless, and the last was peaceful. The first was compelling directive, the last was sweetly persuasive.

God, Bob mentally prayed, *what can I do? It all seems so hopeless. I don't really want to die, but there is nothing worth living for either.* Now, the room was filled with an awesome power, and the quietly persuasive voice became authoritatively strong. Booming into his spirit and leading his mind came the words, "I am worth living for, Bob!"

Page after page from his life scrolled by. Bob saw his whole life as though on a screen. Broken, and in humility, he cried out, *God, what do You want me to do? I can't see what use I am to You, but I'm listening. If You want to talk with me, I'm here.*

As Bob waited before God, his heart finally was led to accept whatever was in the divine plan for the rest of his life. Tears of genuine relief welled up into his eyes. Bob's mind grasped for two words, and as though he was actually speaking them, he said them over and over again: *I'm sorry, I'm sorry, I'm so very sorry.*

A miracle of grace was actually being performed in Robert Jimenez Gutierrez by the Spirit of God. As much as was possible in his weakened condition, he fell prostrate and cried, *God, I really am grateful for the gift of life, and I will try to be something for You.*

The miracle of brokenness was just a prelude to another miracle. It was the miracle of understanding. From the days of his youth, the Holy Spirit gave back to Bob a scriptural promise. Despite his physical discomfort, Bob was virtually entranced before God as the Holy Spirit seemed to trumpet the words: "Call unto Me and I will answer thee, and show thee great and might things which thou knowest not" (Jeremiah 33:3).

Bob reflected, *God, I am calling on Your name. They have told me that I'll never talk, sing, or eat again, so I will call upon Your name. You are real, God, and I believe that there must be some future for me. If there wasn't, then You would have let me die when I first begged death from You.*

With his personal effects all packed and ready to go, there was nothing that hindered Bob from leaving the hospital. While the doctor's judgments were without change, while humanly, Bob had no valid expectations for the future, notwithstanding, he planned to walk out of the institution in the strength of back-to-back miracles. He would walk out in spiritual dependence and brokenness and with a new understanding concerning God's power and might.

In such a manner, and with such expectations, Bob walked out of the room that had been his home for fifteen months. He walked into an unknown future with a certain poise, and even a little spring in his step.

World, I don't know whether you are ready for me, but here I come! he opined.

As Bob's family walked him out of the hospital, they joined their hearts with him and believed for the future, whatever it held.

15

THE DUMB MAN SPOKE

Going home was for Bob much like an old-time homecoming week. Neighbors and friends descended upon the house to express their joy, and yet when they left, they invariably shook their heads in dismay. Whatever time they spent with Bob was an emotional hassle, and one man told his wife, "Don't ask me to go back. The guy cannot answer, cannot eat, and spends most of his time wiping off the saliva from his chin. Sure, I'm glad he made it, but I cannot see to what end. It seems it would have been better for him to have gone to be with the Lord."

With the gut-level intuition of the ill, Bob was aware of such reactions, even though friends were most careful to not show real feelings. Perhaps it was the extreme care, which his visitors used, that gave Bob the inner consciousness of their sensitivity.

For the first six months, Bob refused to go out. He tried to joke around with his family, but those efforts soon paled, and he began to withdraw into himself. He had, by no means, forgotten the last hour at the hospital. The miracle of brokenness and the miracle of understanding were live memories, and in the long night hours, he rethought them many times.

God, I'm not quitting calling out to You. I am sure of Your promise. You said, great and mighty things! God, when are You going to do those things, for my life is useless in its present form!

Bob knew that he had achieved a higher spiritual plane than at any previous time in his life, but he was not able to understand the promises of the angel-lady, and the confirmation of them from Jeremiah 33:3. He figured that what God said, God would do. He simply continued to mentally register, *I'm calling on You, God. I'm calling on You*, and settled in for the long wait. He was grateful for legs and arms that functioned normally, for good eyes and good ears. There were many blessings to be enjoyed, and for which to praise God while he waited on the fulfillment of the promises.

Every day of his life, Bob used a whole box of Kleenex. The saliva in his mouth was a constant source of embarrassment, for it dribbled out ceaselessly. His mother said, "Don't worry about it, Bob. As long as you keep wiping it off, it will not look messy."

"But, Mama," Bob wrote, "God said it was going to be all right. Do you think God will heal me?"

Bob's mother answered with confidence, "If God said He will heal you, then He will heal you."

Bob had never heard such a thing from God. The angelic messenger promised that everything would be all right and had encouraged him to be patient. Bob had interpreted the promise of Jeremiah as an indication that great and mighty things would yet happen to him, but the fact remained, no specific promise had been given to him that he would be healed.

Despite the lack of specificity, Bob believed God for a miracle that would restore his voice. Each night as he called to God, he reminded Him of His promise and assured the Lord that he intended to sing again in the service of the Lord Jesus Christ.

I'm going to sing again! Enemy, do you hear me? I'm going to sing again! Bob's mind was constantly phrasing such faithful statements. No one heard them on earth, but for sure they were heard in heaven, and as it eventuated, they were heard in hell too.

One night, in the middle of his mental faith exercises, he was made aware of a frightening presence in his room. The flow of his praying was closed off, and he was unable to register accurate thoughts to God. Bob opened his eyes and saw in great detail a huge figure lying over him. The figure reached down and, with massive, hairy hands, seized his throat. Bob was petrified in fear. The demonic apparition blazed in hatred at him, and Bob knew in his spirit that what shrapnel had failed to do, Satan was now about to perfect.

The eyes of the demon were huge and bloodshot, and he laughed obscenely as the pressure grew on Bob's throat. Bob pushed and shoved but could not move the hands that held his throat. When he realized that he was making no impression on the evil power, he recognized it for what it was. Satan was going to close his mouth forever, and he knew in a blinding insight that his healing must have been scheduled on God's calendar; Satan did not want him to ever speak or sing again. Across his mind ran a moving picture. In it, he was singing the gospel of Jesus Christ.

Incredible, transforming faith rose in Bob. With all the power of his mental lungs, he screamed to God, *God, I plead the blood of Jesus. I plead the blood of Jesus. Jesus, please help me!*

Suddenly, the pressure was gone, the image disappeared, and Bob jumped out of bed. He looked under his bed, in the closet, and outside his door. He found nothing, for the power of Jesus's blood had triumphed. In that moment, he knew with some divine insight that total healing was on the way. Why else would the enemy have tried to kill him?

Back in his bed, Bob began to worship and praise God. His heart was lifted up within him. *I'm going to be healed . . . healed . . . healed!*

It was now three and a half years since he was wounded in Vietnam. Important spiritual truths became sharp and clear. He had been spared in the original wounding, he saw now, for the glory of God. Against all logical evaluation, he had lived. There had to be a good reason. An angelic messenger had appeared to him on two occasions, urging him to be patient, and had so stopped him from taking his own life. God must have had a good reason for that too. God had brought to his remembrance the promise of His word, and so assured him of the future. Finally, the blood of Jesus was strong to protect him against demonic attack.

I feel loved! he silently screamed. He shouted so loudly that if he had possessed a voice, the entire neighborhood would have been awakened. Over and over, he shouted, *I'm going to be healed! I'm going to be healed!* The way Bob saw it, there was no other way it could be. God, he figured, was bringing him through.

Many of the things, which were occurring in Bob, he did not share with his family. They were things that were very private, just between God, the Heavenly Father, and Robert Jimenez Gutierrez.

In fact, Bob had begun to feel like some bomb, wired for detonation. The conviction grew each day that God was going to heal him. He spent much time rehearsing the physical impossibility of such a thing taking place. He knew that the twelfth cranial nerve was wholly gone. At the base of his tongue, there was no way existing whereby even a slight movement could be achieved. The twelfth cranial nerve was the means by which any tongue movement originated.

So, God, he ruminated, *You will have to make a new twelfth cranial! I sure don't know how You will do it, but You must either do that, or devise an alternate means by which I swallow, speak, and sing. I believe You are going to heal me, because of what Your Son did at the cross.*

God, I need You to heal me soon. I want to get on with my work for Jesus. OK?

One morning, Bob awoke to a strange sensation. He became aware of some slight feeling at the very base of his tongue. It was, indeed, only a sensation of feeling, not distinct, but tantalizingly real. He cried out to God, *Please let something be happening. God, I believe You are going to heal me . . . I believe!*

Every instinct in him told Bob that the trial of his faith was almost over. He was weary of putting all his food through a blender and creating thin liquid drinks, drinks by which he lived. He was weary of going to his bedroom and awkwardly pouring fluids down his throat. He was weary of not swallowing or talking. In Bob's mind, it was time for faith's fruit to be seen.

Bob did not at first speak to his family with regard to the ever-so-slight feeling. Each day he was increasingly conscious that something was, indeed, happening. He began to be excited.

One morning, the unthinkable, impossible took shape. Bob's mother walked into his room, and as she entered, a mighty surge of spiritual force shook Bob. A huge impulse stirred, moving from his mind into his entire body. He opened his mouth and knew he could move his tongue. The slab of meat followed the command of his mind, and Bob spoke! Tens of thousands of words had passed through his mind in the anguishing period of time since April 15, 1969, but not one of them had the significance of the first word that came from him at that moment.

Bob, like a little baby, said, "Mama."

When the first excitement passed, Bob's next word was, "Papa." The twentieth-century miracle was, to Bob, the shot that was heard around the world.

16

NOT ASHAMED!

God had indeed given Bob back the ability to speak. With the twelfth cranial nerve wholly gone and with the additional serious lacerations to the vocal chords that left permanent damage, there was no humanly way by which Bob would, or could, speak again. The medical judgment was that all normal functions of the mouth, tongue, and throat were permanently gone. Yet this man spoke!

Bob was overwhelmed with gratitude to God, and as his ability to speak grew, so did his longing to serve the Lord Jesus Christ. "I've got to begin to serve Him," were common words from his lips, until they sounded like a broken record. Day by day, his speech improved. In fact, he was learning to speak all over again, and his own way to describe his development indicated that he felt like he was a baby. After all, he had been totally silent for three and a half years.

Within a short time, Bob was laboring with a group of young singers. He was still too sensitive in regard to his speech development to give his testimony in public, but while he waited for the more perfect ability, he wrote his testimony and allowed other team members to read it.

During those days, a pastor in Modesto, California, heard the testimony read. He became deeply interested in Bob's story, and he was the means of getting Bob on radio and television. Despite the passion he had to serve God, Bob was reluctant to speak himself, fearing that those who listened would not be able to hear him clearly enough. God's miracle for Bob was of the same nature as that recorded of a blind man in Mark's gospel; it came by degrees, but it did come!

Along with God's creative gift of speech and tongue movement came the thrilling experience of learning to eat again! As with his speech, so it was with his eating. He had to learn to do it all over again, but he did learn. The day came when Bob would eat comfortably. He was ready to launch himself into normal living, and with great excitement, he went back to Bible College, this time in El Paso, Texas. The man whom the United States Army said would never be normal was, by supernatural power, ready to enter the service of the Lord Jesus Christ.

During the time when Bob was adjusting to his wonderful new life, the Holy Spirit was also working in the heart and life of a beautiful young lady in Michigan. There were two things Linda wanted in life. She longed to attend Bible College, and she prayed that God would lead her in life to be joined in marriage with somebody with whom she could serve Jesus Christ. In her prayerful enquiries about a Christian education, she was induced to apply for admission to the same school to which Bob had been accepted.

Boy meets girl—*un Latino y una Latina*! The attractions were mutual and immediate, but the young lady from Michigan had determined in her heart that only a real man of God could win her. A miracle out of Vietnam was not, by itself, enough for her. Linda had asked God for the best, and she was determined to test this man. "I will put a fleece out like Gideon did," she said. It certainly did not matter to her that some theologians had seen

Gideon's action as lack of faith! Her desire was to know beyond any doubt concerning this man, and to Linda, it was pure faith on her part.

"Heavenly Father," she prayed, "if he is Your man for my life, let him ask me to 'go steady.'" In the autumn of 1972, "going steady" was almost a commitment, and it precluded either party from dating anybody else. Linda's "fleece" was a tough test, for the evening before she prayed, they had agreed casually that "going steady" was not what Christians should do, a fairly common viewpoint in evangelical circles at the time.

Linda waited and prayed. Bob also prayed, but he found it very hard to wait! He just knew that Linda was the girl with whom he wished to spend the rest of his life. With his heart in his hands, he determined to ask Linda if they could "go steady."

Linda said, "Let me pray about it."

When Linda was alone with God, she searched her heart and her motivation. "I've got to be sure, Lord," she prayed. "I mean, I have to be really sure!" Linda decided to put out another "fleece." "After all, Gideon made two efforts, and I will, too," she reasoned.

"Father, if it was just a coincidence, I need to know. If Bob is really the man You want me to marry, then have him tell me immediately that he loves me." Linda knew that in secular thinking, "going steady" was usually for a length of time during which a man and a woman could discover whether they loved one another. She was short-circuiting normal practice!

Bob was also talking with God. "Tell her you love her and want to marry her!" was what he heard. He also knew what was normal practice, but once again, he put his heart in his hands, and with some trepidation, he told Linda that he loved her, and he said, "I want to marry you."

Linda decided to outdistance Gideon. "Lord, I hear You, but in this one thing, I can't afford to be wrong. Please speak to me about Bob."

During the night, the Lord came to Linda in a strong dream vision. In the dream, she and Bob were being married. The beautiful white gown was emblematic of the purity that was in her heart. In the morning, she rose with a total conviction that Robert Jimenez Gutierrez was not only the man she must marry, but was also the man she wished to marry.

The initial, instant attraction that each had felt for the other had blossomed into a mature love. A love that was enhanced and magnified by the love they both had for the Lord Jesus Christ.

Bob and Linda became husband and wife on December 27, 1972. With resolution and great joy, they turned their hearts toward the service of the Master.

17

SERVING THE KING OF KINGS

When Linda married Bob Gutierrez, she knew that she had married more than the man. With her eyes of faith, she had seen the pattern of the future and, with no evasion of mind, accepted whatever it held. Linda and Bob not only had a common love for Jesus Christ, but they also enjoyed common belief in the anointing power of the Holy Spirit. They both saw their lives as being wholly at the disposal of their Master, and they were willing to pay whatever price the commitment implied.

They were married in the little town of Flat Rock, Michigan, and from that place, they asked the Lord for directions for their future service. They knew what they should expect if they were moving in the power of the Holy Spirit. Bob loved to think back upon one of the occasions when God had confirmed the nature of the work that would be the standard for the future. He had conducted a service on the campus of the Bible College in which he had recently been a student. That night, the power of God fell on the people like a baseball-sized hailstorm. There was a localized revival what many old-timers called a Holy Ghost revival. People were still in the auditorium at midnight, and God, who had given Bob back his voice, had used it mightily. The quality of his speech had developed phenomenally, and along with such miraculous proof of God's presence, the beautiful singing ability of his pre-Vietnam wounding came right along with his voice.

Bob and Linda knew that the pattern was set for the years that were ahead. They would sing and preach, both to the Christians and to those who were not. They had no idea as to how their ministry might open and develop, but they had the faith to believe that the One who had called them would also provide opportunities for their service.

In the early years of their ministry, Bob and Linda gladly accepted lives of faith, and many times did not know from where their next meal would come. They lived out of a little Volkswagen, constantly seeking God for another place in which to minister.

In Detroit, Michigan, Bob began the adventure of full-time service for Christ. He did so in a way that most certainly would not have seemed practical to more mature pastors and evangelists. He said to Linda, "I'm going to check the yellow pages and call some of the listed churches!" It was an original idea, but when he came to do it, he had no answer to the question as to which church, or churches, to call.

Bob looked at the pages of churches and went blank. "Which church should I call?" he asked Linda. There were Baptist and Christian churches, Catholic and Episcopalian, Methodist and Presbyterian, Lutheran and Pentecostal churches, and numerous other groups. It could be supposed that somehow his eyes gravitated to a page of churches that would have some like-mindedness, but at some point in his struggle, he said, "I'm going to close my eyes and put my finger down on the page. I will call the church upon which my finger lands!"

Bob closed his eyes, dropped his finger, and then called a little Detroit church. Stumblingly, he spoke to the pastor. "My name is

Bob Gutierrez, and I came out of Vietnam as a permanent mute. They actually tied a 'dead' tag on me originally. I not only lived, but God gave me back my professional singing voice, and now I am telling the story of his miracle power in my life. I would like to come and share my story with your people."

That first call made history. The pastor agreed for Bob to sing and share. The occasion was a kind of first fruit. Soon, pastors and people began to tell others of this man with the incredible story, and the ministry of Robert Jimenez Gutierrez was off and flying, accompanied by signs and wonders.

Typical of the sensational impact of Bob's story was an authentic incident that developed while he was in Puerto Rico. As might have been expected, the miracle of a Hispanic soldier was sufficient to stir much interest. Among those who were impacted was an imminent laryngology specialist, Dr. Anibal Navarro Badui. As a man of science, he was not prepared to accept the miracle. The doctor was a devoted Christian, and as such, he could accept the truth that God could do anything He wished. In Bob's case, he requested the opportunity to conduct a full examination. His study became so intense that he finally examined Bob four times.

After the first examination, he left shaking his head. Later, he phoned. "Would you mind if I took another look at your throat?"

"Of course not," Bob replied.

After the second examination, he called yet again, asking for a third opportunity. Bob smiled, and once again assented. After the third examination, Dr. Anibal Navarro Badui phoned again, requesting a fourth and final look at this walking miracle.

Four examinations later, the doctor participated in the filming of a videotape concerning Bob, the precursor of this book. With full anatomical charts, he detailed the exact injury as recorded in the military medical reports.

Dr. Badui said, "When I had completed my full examinations of our beloved brother Bob, I found that not only did the shrapnel effect a wound that should have killed him, but following his survival, there could never be any known way for surgical corrections. Despite this, he is able to use his tongue to speak, to sing, and to swallow, and all of this without the nerve which creates lingual movement.

"Additionally," the doctor said, "I discovered that Brother Bob has been given two entirely new vocal chords, and there is no indication on them that they were ever injured!"

Some time into their ministry, Bob and Linda were able to buy a small five-wheel trailer and a truck. Life became somewhat easier, and in those days, the Lord gave to them two lovely children. Lynette was born on January 29, 1974; Robert, who would always be known as B. J., was born on November 23, 1975. Bob grew a truly handsome beard and moustache, and the combination gave him an air of mature sophistication.

The children displayed a true musical capacity from their earliest years. They began to sing children's songs at the ages of five and three.

The years flew by. The "must die! can't live! grunt," the Mexican American soldier whose life and future had been wholly demolished by a rocket fragment on April 15, 1969, became a living witness of the grace and healing virtue of the Lord Jesus Christ. In the battle for survival, God won. Because He won, Robert Jimenez Gutierrez won also. With his wife by his side, and his talented adult teenagers in tandem, the singing four made a national impact.

Bob had been tagged dead, but he lived. He was dumb, but he spoke. He called to the Lord, and was heard. He lost his voice to gain another. He almost had his name on the Vietnam Memorial in Washington DC, but the Lord allowed it to be seen in hundreds of locations, in most states of the country, and abroad. In Israel, Mexico, Puerto Rico, and elsewhere, the Gutierrez family still continues to leave its mark for Jesus Christ, and Bob is a seasoned warrior in a better war than that which almost killed him.

Blessed be the name of the Lord!

A PERSONAL MESSAGE FROM BOB GUTIERREZ

Dear Reader:

Thank you so much for reading the story of my life. It is my fervent prayer that it blessed you. Remember, you can receive the mercy of the Lord, as did I. Jesus Christ can save you, keep you, and heal you. I want to ask you to put your faith in Him.

If this book has blessed you, or if as a result of reading it you desire to know more about Christ, I urge you to write me a note. I am available to you. My address is:

Bob Gutierrez Ministries
2602 Oxford Oaks Lane
Corinth, TX 76210
Telephone: 940-230-6499

I am also available to come to your church. It would be a privilege to share the ministry of the Lord with you.

Bob Gutierrez

INDEX

calling on, 86

carried the peace of, 43

caused another vision, 67

fellowship with, 21

heard by, 28

Kingdom of, 30

other men who loved, 36

pleading for death from, 75

touch of, 27

voice given by, 47

wrestled with, 81

See also King of Kings

grace, 83

Gutierrez, Linda, 15

Gutierrez, Mike, 27, 63-64

Gutierrez, Nieves, 19-21, 31, 33, 38

Gutierrez, Paul, 27

Gutierrez, Ramon, 19-21, 23, 31, 33, 38

Gutierrez, Robert "Bob" Jimenez, 15, 73, 78, 83, 94

birth of, 19-21

teenage years, 24-27

founding of own gospel quartet, 29

joining the army, 31-38

in Vietnam, 39-67, 69, 81, 88, 92, 96-97, 99

singing in the army, 42-44, 48, 50

singing in the Bob Hope Christmas special, 49-50

incurring injury, 63-67

pronounced dead, 69, 72

undergoing treatment, 73-79

encounter with Satan, 86

regaining ability to speak, 91

Gutierrez, Xavier, 23, 27, 74

H

Holy Ghost revival, 95

Holy spirit, 33, 83, 92

anointing power of the, 95

dependence on the power of the, 28

Hope, Bob, 49

J

Jesus Christ, 24, 33-34, 43, 87, 89, 91-92, 94-95, 98-99

deeply committed to, 21

pleading the blood of, 87

understanding the pain and suffering of, 67

wanted to serve, 29

will only sing for, 28, 50, 87

win people to, 15

K

King of Kings, 30, 34. *See also* God

L

Latin American Bible College, 15, 29, 31, 92, 95

lieutenant, 41

London, Eddie (jazz star), 48-50

M

Mike Douglas Show, 63-64
ministry, 15, 29, 97-98
  early years of, 96
miracle, 28, 48, 83, 85-86, 92, 97
music, 21, 27, 29, 43, 49-50
  for the troops, 47

N

nerves, 75, 77, 98
  twelfth cranial, 70, 88-89, 91

O

"Oh, Holy Night," 50

P

patience, 79

R

Rolling stones, 47

S

san Joaquin College, 32
satan, 28, 87
scrgcant, 40, 42, 59-60
soldiers, 17, 30, 34, 40, 42-43, 49, 55, 57, 59, 76
Steve (Bob's friend), 63-65
  death of, 65

U

United states Army, 17, 31-32, 37, 40
  ready to be a soldier in the, 34
    turbulent months before induction to the, 47

V

Vietcong, 55, 60, 64
  breached the perimeter of Camp Enari, 65
    constant intrusion of the, 69
    struggle was in favor of the, 57
Vietnam War, 18, 37, 40, 44, 52, 55, 60, 69
    American solder caught up in the, 47
  calling men for the, 36
  result of the horror of the, 78
  was unlike any war, 57